P9-CAN-295

12/08

EDGE
BOOKS

MAGIC TRICKS

CAPSTONE PRESS PRESENTS

AMAZING

MAGIC

TRICKS

EXPERT

LEVEL

by NORM BARNHART

Capstone
press®

Mankato, Minnesota

Edge Books are published by Capstone Press,
151 Good Counsel Drive, P.O. Box 669, Mankato, Minnesota 56002.
www.capstonepress.com

Library of Congress Cataloging-in-Publication Data
Barnhart, Norm.
    Amazing magic tricks: expert level / by Norm Barnhart.
    p. cm. — (Edge books. Magic Tricks.)
    Includes bibliographical references and index.
    Summary: "Step-by-step instructions and clear photos describe how to
perform magic tricks at the expert level" — Provided by publisher.
    ISBN-13: 978-1-4296-1945-5 (hardcover)
    ISBN-10: 1-4296-1945-7 (hardcover)
    1. Magic tricks — Juvenile literature. I. Title. II. Series.
GV1548.B354 2009
793.8 — dc22   2008002574

Editorial Credits
Aaron Sautter, editor; Bob Lentz, designer/illustrator; Marcy Morin, scheduler

Photo Credits
Capstone Press/Karon Dubke, cover, objects, magic steps
Shutterstock/Chen-Ping Hung; javarman; Marilyn Volan;
    Tatiana53; Tischenko Irina, backgrounds

Capstone Press thanks Anthony Wacholtz of Compass Point Books and
Hilary Wacholz of Picture Window Books for their help in producing this book.

1 2 3 4 5 6 13 12 11 10 09 08

TABLE OF CONTENTS

BOOK
3

INCREDIBLE MAGIC!

Magicians are storytellers. They weave wild tales about strange places and mysterious people while they perform their fantastic tricks. In these pages you'll learn several tricks to astound your family and friends. You can add your own clever stories to keep your audience entertained. It's time to learn some incredible magic!

THE KEYS TO MAGIC

→ Practice, practice, practice! If you want your tricks to work right, you need to practice until you can do them quickly and smoothly. Try standing in front of a mirror while practicing. Then you can see what the tricks will look like to your audience.

→ Keep it secret! Magicians never share their secrets. If you reveal the secrets of a trick, people won't be very impressed. It also ruins the trick for other magicians who want to do it in the future.

→ Be entertaining! Try telling the audience some jokes or stories that relate to your tricks while performing them. Keep the audience entertained and they won't notice how the tricks are done. It will also keep them coming back for more.

BEFORE YOU BEGIN

Most magicians hide their props in a magic box. A magic box will help you keep your tricks organized and your special props hidden from the audience. You can make your own magic box. Find a cardboard box and decorate it with some colorful stars, or cover it with dark cloth so it looks mysterious.

A magic wand is one of a magician's most useful tools. Wands help direct people's attention to what you want them to see. You can make a wand out of a wooden dowel painted black and white. Or roll up a piece of black construction paper and tape the ends. You can add sparkles and stars if you wish. Be creative and have fun!

A MAGIC SECRET - THE DITCH

The Ditch, or secret drop, is one of the most valuable secrets in magic. The audience thinks you're grabbing your magic wand. But at the same time, you secretly drop a hidden object into your magic box. Don't look stiff or nervous while you do this. Just act calm while you smoothly make the switch. The audience won't suspect a thing!

THE MAGIC HANKY

Lots of people carry hankies in case they have to sneeze. Where do you think magicians keep their hankies? With this fun trick, you can make a colorful hanky appear from an empty paper bag!

WHAT YOU NEED:

* A colorful handkerchief
* Two small paper bags
* Colorful confetti

PREPARATION:

1. For this trick, you'll need a secret pocket in the bottom of a paper bag. To make it, cut the top half off of one paper bag. Keep the bottom half and set it to the side.

2. Next, place the hanky at the bottom of the second bag. Then place the half bag inside the whole bag on top of the hanky. The hanky is now hidden inside the secret pocket. Now it's time to trick the audience!

3. First, tell the audience about your magic confetti that can create a new hanky any time you need one. Next, pick up the bag and show the audience that it's empty by turning it upside down. Ask a volunteer to stick a hand in the bag to make sure it's empty.

4. Now toss some of the colorful confetti into the bag. Wave your wand over the bag and say a few magic words.

Next, blow the bag up like a balloon. Then twist the top and pop it so the confetti flies out as shown.

5. After startling the audience with the loud bang, it's time to amaze them by pulling out the colorful hanky. Say something like, "Magic confetti is great. It works every time!"

magic tip: If you have a rainbow-colored hanky, have the audience pretend to take a tiny pinch of color off their shirts and toss it toward the bag. Then a rainbow-colored hanky amazingly appears!

7

SUNDAY COMICS HERO

People love reading the Sunday comic pages. Everybody has a favorite character. You can make your favorite character appear out of nowhere with this fun trick!

WHAT YOU NEED:

→ Color comics from a Sunday newspaper
→ A small toy figure
→ Glue

PREPARATION:

1. First, glue the comics together to make a secret pocket as shown.

2. Then hide the small toy figure inside the secret pocket. A thin, flat toy works best so the audience doesn't see that something is hidden inside.

3. First, hold up the Sunday comics and show them to the audience. Tell them a story about your favorite character. Mention how you love the character's adventures or how the character always makes you laugh. Be sure to keep the secret pocket hidden.

4. Tell the audience that the character sometimes likes to come out and say, "Hello." Then roll the paper into a cone shape so the secret pocket is in the middle. Next, wave your magic wand over the cone and say a few magic words.

5. Finally, reach into the cone and pull out the toy figure. Have the toy take a bow as the audience gives you a round of applause!

magic tip: You can do this trick with a comic book too. Make a secret pocket by gluing a second back cover onto a comic book. Then just roll the comic book into a tube and let the toy slide out into your hand.

MAGIC MAG-NEE-TO MAN

Astonish your friends with your magical magnetic powers! Become the Magical Mag-Nee-To Man and make a plastic cup stick like a magnet to a book. It's an easy gravity-defying trick.

WHAT YOU NEED:

* A plastic cup
* A book
* A paper clip

PREPARATION:

1. First, bend one end of the paper clip so it sticks straight out. Then hold it against the book with your thumb as shown.

2. Now place the cup over the paper clip and press it against the paper clip with your thumb. This is the secret of the trick. With enough practice, you'll be able to hold the book at any angle and the cup should stay in place.

3. First, rub the cup against your hair. While you do this say, "People tell me I have a magnetic personality. And they're right. I can affect objects with my magnetic power!"

4. Now get the book and paper clip from your magic box. Hold up the book and show it to the audience. Be sure they can't see that you are holding the paper clip behind the book. Then place the cup over the paper clip as shown.

5. Firmly hold the cup against the book like you practiced earlier. Then slowly turn the book over to show that the cup is stuck to it. Take a bow as the audience applauds your incredible magnetic abilities!

magic tip: Try ending the trick by pretending that the cup is stuck to the book so well that you can't get it off. This will add some fun comedy for the audience.

4

THE ESCAPING COIN

Big or small, all magic tricks are just illusions. Sometimes the best illusions are when the magic happens right in a person's hand. This one will leave the whole audience baffled!

WHAT YOU NEED:

→ Seven pennies

PERFORMANCE:

1. First, tell the audience that money sometimes has a mind of its own and likes to escape. Pick up the pennies one at a time and place them in your left hand. Count them out loud so the audience knows how many there are.

2. Now ask a volunteer to hold out his or her hand. Count out loud as you transfer the coins, one at a time, from your hand into the volunteer's hand.

3. When you get to the sixth penny, tap it against the coins in the volunteer's hand as shown. The sound will cause the volunteer and the audience to believe that it landed with the other coins.

4. Instead of giving the volunteer the sixth penny, simply keep it hidden in your right hand. This will take practice so the volunteer doesn't see that you keep it. Now drop the last penny into the volunteer's hand as shown. Ask your volunteer to close his or her hand tightly so no coins can escape.

Hidden coin

5. Put your hand hiding the secret penny under the volunteer's hand in a fist as shown. Bump the volunteer's hand a couple of times, then let the hidden coin drop into your left hand as shown. Finally, ask the volunteer to count out the number of coins he or she has in their hand. When the volunteer counts only six coins, the audience will think the coin escaped right through your volunteer's closed hand!

THE ZOOMING MOON ROCK

Even rocks can get homesick. Here's a trick you can use to send a lonely moon rock zooming back home to the moon. Everybody will be left wondering how it's done!

WHAT YOU NEED:

→ A small, shiny rock
→ Two foam cups
→ A scissors

PREPARATION:

1. First, make a secret hole by cutting out the bottom of one foam cup with the scissors as shown.

2. Next, stack the cups so the cup with the secret hole is on the bottom. Then put the rock in the top cup as shown.

3. First, ask a volunteer in the audience to help you with this trick. Dump the moon rock into the volunteer's hand and ask him or her to show it to the audience. Then tell the audience a story about magical moon rocks that fly home to the moon when they get lonely.

4. Now separate the cups. Be sure to hide the secret hole by keeping that cup in the palm of your hand as shown. Tell the audience that you're going to send the rock home with some help from your volunteer. Then have the volunteer put the rock back in the normal cup.

Secret hole

5. Next, place the two cups together mouth to mouth as shown.

 TURN PAGE FOR MORE!

15

6. Tip over the cups so the rock falls through the secret hole and into your hand as shown. Be sure to keep the hole covered with your hand so the audience won't see it.

7. Next, set the cups on the table so they are stacked mouth to mouth as shown. Be sure to keep the rock hidden in your hand.

Hidden rock

8. Now get your magic wand out of your magic box. As you reach into the box, leave the rock behind as shown.

9. Here's where the magic happens! Wave your magic wand over the stacked cups. You can ask your volunteer to repeat some magic words to help send the rock home too. Then pretend to watch the rock zoom home to the moon.

10. Finally, slam your hand down on the stacked cups to smash them up. Tear up the pieces to show that the rock has disappeared into outer space! Thank the volunteer and ask your audience to give him or her a round of applause!

magic tip: Try having the volunteer wave the magic wand over the cups. He or she will be astounded that the rock disappeared!

THE TRICKY LEPRECHAUN

Leprechauns are real pranksters. The audience will be amazed when an invisible leprechaun steals a coin. Then they'll have a good laugh when you find it hiding in your shoe!

WHAT YOU NEED:

→ Two identical coins
→ A colorful handkerchief
→ A shirt with a chest pocket
→ A tissue

PREPARATION:

1. First, place the tissue into the bottom of your shirt pocket as shown. This helps keep it open a bit. Then hide one of the coins in your shoe.

PERFORMANCE:

2. Start by telling the audience a story about a tricky, invisible leprechaun that likes to steal coins and hide them. Then hold up the second coin in your left hand and show it to the audience. Hold the hanky in your right hand.

3. Now drag the hanky over your hand and the coin. As you do this, take the coin in your right hand as shown. Be sure to keep the coin behind the hanky so the audience can't see it.

4. As you drag the hanky toward you, secretly drop the coin into your shirt pocket as shown. Keep looking at your empty hand under the hanky so the audience doesn't suspect anything.

5. Once the coin is hidden, pull away the hanky to show that the coin has disappeared! Act surprised at how fast that tricky Leprechaun is. Than start searching for the coin. Pretend to check your pockets and in your magic box. Finally, take off the shoe holding the secret coin. The audience will be amazed that the leprechaun hid the coin there!

magic tip: Try hiding the secret coin under a chair in the audience instead of inside your shoe. When the coin disappears, ask them to look for it under their chairs. When someone finds it, they can keep it as a gift!

MULTIPLYING MONEY

Everybody likes having plenty of money. Magic with money really grabs people's attention. This trick will make the audience wish their money could multiply this fast!

WHAT YOU NEED:

- Six coins
- Two popsicle sticks
- Tape
- A table and chair

PREPARATION:

1. First, create a secret pocket by taping the popsicle sticks to the bottom of the table as shown. The space between them should be a little smaller than the coins are wide. Be sure the pocket is near the side of the table you'll be sitting at.

2. Next, slide one or two coins into the secret pocket made by the popsicle sticks. The gap between the sticks should allow you to easily get at the coins.

3. Start by laying out the rest of the coins on the table. Tell your audience, "Making money is easy. I can make these coins multiply." Ask a volunteer to count the coins on the table.

4. Now slide the coins off the edge of the table with one hand so they drop into your other hand.

5. At the same time, use your second hand to slide a coin out of the secret pocket as shown.

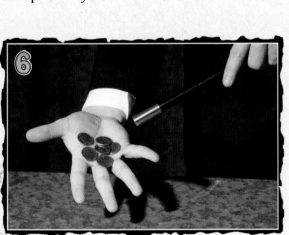

6. Close your hand around the coins, then wave your magic wand over your hand in a mystical way and say a few magic words. Finally, open your hand and have the volunteer recount the coins. The audience will be stunned when they see that the coins have multiplied!

THE MYSTIC SNOWFLAKE

No two snowflakes are exactly alike. With this trick you can make a paper snowflake with special magical scissors. The audience won't believe their eyes when it magically appears!

WHAT YOU NEED:

→ A scissors
→ Two sheets of paper

PREPARATION:

1. First, fold one sheet of paper in half three or four times. Then cut a few pieces out around the edges as shown to make a paper snowflake.

PERFORMANCE:

2. Leave the paper snowflake folded up. When you're ready to do the trick, take the plain paper out of your magic box. At the same time, hide the paper snowflake in your hand as shown.

Snowflake

3. Tell the audience you can make a snowflake with magic invisible scissors. Show them the plain paper and fold it three or four times. With the final fold, secretly switch the plain paper with the snowflake. Hide the plain paper in the palm of your hand. Be sure the audience doesn't see you switch the two pieces of paper.

Snowflake

Hidden paper

4. Next, use the hand that is hiding the plain paper to reach into your pocket for your magic invisible scissors. Leave the paper behind in your pocket.

5. Now pretend to pull out the magic invisible scissors. Use your fingers like scissors as shown, and pretend to cut out a paper snowflake.

6. Finally, unfold the paper snowflake and show it to the audience. They will be amazed when they see that the paper has been transformed right before their eyes!

THE CRAZY COMICAL SOCK

The best way to warm up an audience is to get them laughing. With this trick, the audience gets a good laugh when you find something you didn't even know was lost!

WHAT YOU NEED:

→ Two identical socks
→ A piece of black cloth
→ A black hat
→ Four safety pins

1

PREPARATION:

1. First, pin the black cloth into the bottom of the hat to create a secret pocket as shown. Then tuck a sock into the secret pocket.

2. Next, put the other sock on your left foot. Leave your right foot bare under your shoe as shown.

2

3. Start by telling the audience that you often find the strangest things in your hat. Say, "I never know what I might get when I do this trick." Then hold the hat up to show the audience that it's empty.

4. Now wave your magic wand over the hat and say a few mysterious magic words.

5. Reach into the hat and pull out the sock. Make a funny, confused look on your face. The audience will think something went wrong.

6. While looking confused, lift your left pant leg to show the matching sock. Then quickly lift your right pant leg to show that the sock is missing. Act surprised or embarrassed — as if you made the sock appear in the hat by mistake. The audience will have a good laugh and enjoy the rest of the show!

THE MAGIC PENNY BANK

Do you like saving your pennies? Now you can save money in a bottle without even removing the top. Your audience will be astounded when a coin seems to appear out of nowhere!

WHAT YOU NEED:

- A plastic juice bottle
- 3 pennies with the same date
- A colorful handkerchief
- Tape

PREPARATION:

1. First, place a small loop of tape inside the bottle's cap. Then lightly place one of the pennies on the tape as shown. Don't press down too hard on the penny or the trick won't work at the end.

2. Ask an adult to help you with this next step. Hide a secret, second penny inside a secret pocket in the hanky. Do this by folding the corner of the hanky over the penny and sewing it in place as shown.

3. First, pick up the bottle and show the audience that it's empty. Tell them that you like to save your extra coins, but that you hate having to open the top all the time. Then gently screw on the top. Be sure the hidden penny doesn't fall into the bottle.

4. Put the bottle down and pick up the third penny. Say, "I like saving my coins by magic instead." Then pretend to place the penny in the center of the hanky. Instead of the third penny, you will really hold the secret penny hidden inside the hanky as shown. Hide the third penny in the palm of your hand.

Secret penny

5. Now ask a volunteer to hold the penny in the hanky. He or she will actually hold the secret penny hidden in the hanky. Be sure to keep the third penny hidden.

TURN PAGE FOR MORE!

27

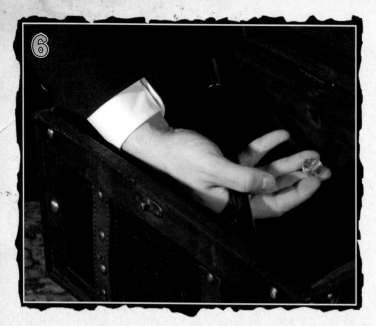

6. Get your magic wand out of your magic box. Drop the hidden third penny into the box as you pick up the wand as shown.

7. Next, wave your magic wand over the hanky and say a few magic words. Then quickly pull the hanky out of the volunteer's hand to show that the penny has vanished!

magic tip: Think of a story to go along with this trick to make it more mysterious and entertaining. Maybe President Lincoln has magical jumping powers. Or maybe the bank belongs to a ghost!

8. Now pick up the bottle and cover it with the hanky. Give the magic wand to the volunteer and ask him or her to wave it over the bottle and say a few magic words. Then tap the bottle firmly against your hand. This should release the secret penny inside the bottle cap so it drops into the bottle. You should hear it rattle inside the bottle.

9. Finally, remove the hanky, open the bottle, and drop the penny into your volunteer's hand. The audience will be amazed at how the coin disappeared from the volunteer's hand and reappeared inside the bottle. Thank the volunteer for helping and ask the audience to give him or her a round of applause!

GLOSSARY

applause (uh-PLAWZ) — clapping hands to show appreciation or approval

audience (AW-dee-uhns) — people who watch or listen to a play, movie, or show

confetti (kuhn-FE-tee) — small pieces of colored paper that people throw at parties, parades, and other celebrations

ditch (DICH) — to secretly switch one object for another

illusion (i-LOO-zhuhn) — something that appears to be real but isn't

leprechaun (LEP-ruh-kawn) — a dwarf or elf in Irish folklore that likes to gather and hide treasure

magnetic (mag-NET-ik) — having the attractive properties of a magnet

prop (PROP) — an item used by an actor or performer during a show

volunteer (vol-uhn-TIHR) — someone who offers to help perform a task during a show

READ MORE

Leeming, Joseph. *Easy Magic Tricks for Kids.* Mineola, N.Y.: Dover, 2008.

Mandelberg, Robert. *Mind-Reading Card Tricks.* New York: Sterling, 2004.

Zenon, Paul. *Cool Card Tricks: Techniques for the Advanced Magician.* Amazing Magic. New York: Rosen, 2008.

INTERNET SITES

FactHound offers a safe, fun way to find Internet sites related to this book. All of the sites on FactHound have been researched by our staff.

Here's how:
1. Visit *www.facthound.com*
2. Choose your grade level.
3. Type in this book ID **1429619457** for age-appropriate sites. You may also browse subjects by clicking on letters, or by clicking on pictures and words.
4. Click on the **Fetch It** button.

FactHound will fetch the best sites for you!

About the author

Norm Barnhart is a professional comic magician who has entertained audiences for more than 28 years. In 2007, Norm was named America's Funniest Magician by the Family Entertainers Workshop. Norm's travels have taken him across the United States and to five other countries. He also loves getting kids excited about reading. Norm says, "I love bringing smiles to people's faces with magic. After reading this book, kids will love doing magic too."